When one door closes, another door opens—but it's

HELL in the HALLWAY

Written and Edited by
SANDI BACHOM

HAZELDEN

Hazelden
Center City, Minnesota 55012-0176

1-800-328-0094
1-651-213-4590 (Fax)
www.hazelden.org

This book is a compilation of aphorisms and reflections, some written by the author, some
quoted from other sources, and some drawn from common parlance.

Library of Congress Cataloging-in-Publication Data

Bachom, Sandi, 1944–
   Hell in the hallway / written and edited by Sandi Bachom.
      p.   cm.
   ISBN-13: 978-1-59285-368-7
   ISBN-10: 1-59285-368-4
      1. Conduct of life—Quotations, maxims, etc. 2. Encouragement—Quotations, maxims,
   etc. 3. Life change events—Quotations, maxims, etc. I. Title.
   BJ1531.B25 2007
   155.9'3—dc22

                                                                    2006050882

11 10 09 08 07   6 5 4 3 2 1

Cover and interior design by David Spohn
Typesetting by Prism Publishing Center

To Dorothy and Jack, my mother and father,
who taught me how to forgive.
To my son Grant, who teaches me how to love.
And to everyone who ever has been, is,
or will be in the hallway.

Contents

Introduction

The hallway. We have all been there after experiencing a major disappointment like a relationship breakup, divorce, job loss, or death of loved one. It can be the loneliest place in the world. But for me, that place of transition, terror, and uncomfortable change is always a source of incubation and healing. I have learned that there is a gift wrapped inside every adversity. I had a dramatic reminder of this in 2001 when I was fifty-seven years old.

On September 10, I did not know it would be the last day of a thirty-year career and my twenty-year marriage. September 10 was also the last day of "normal" for my precious New York City.

Through the grace of God, I had been sober fourteen years on the morning of September 11, and I instinctively knew how to handle situations that used to baffle me. When I went to Chelsea Piers, a triage center for the rescue workers at Ground Zero, to give blood, I ended up staying for a week. I didn't question it. I had learned how to be of service by helping other suffering alcoholics, but I had never volunteered beyond that because I was always too busy working. If I had had a job to go to that day, I would have missed the best work of my life. That week

I became "Sandi Cell Queen," working with others to procure hundreds of phones for rescue workers at Ground Zero who had no other means to communicate with each other.

What I learned that week changed my life forever. I learned that the finest moments are about selfless service and kindness to strangers. Every loss triggers another loss, and I discovered that in our tears and humanness, we are all connected. Amid all the examples of compassion and forgiveness that I witnessed, I saw that the other side of resentment is love. And somehow, if you can offer a small smile and a bit of kindness amid life's greatest horrors, you have the ability to heal.

I learned that if you have faith and hope, you can lose everything and still survive. Resentments will eat you alive, but forgiving the one person you can't forgive will transform you *both*.

When my stepfather was dying and my tumultuous relationship with him was at an end, I traveled to California to see him one last time. It was Yom Kippur, and a Jewish friend had told me that, on this day, you were to beg forgiveness of those you had harmed. I had always thought that I had forgiven him, which I had, but there is a huge distinction between forgiving and begging forgiveness. With my friend's words in my heart, I leaned over and whispered in my stepfather's ear, "Bob, please forgive me." He looked at me with eyes welling, hugged me, and said, "I love you." It was as simple as that. Fifty years of resentment *gone* in three words.

I was reminded of the story of the man who was jailed for many years, counting the days on the wall of his cell until his release. He spent every waking moment planning for the day he would be free. On that joyous day, he went to the door of the cell, heart pounding with anticipation, and discovered that the door had never been locked.

We are all prisoners of our own making. Our will and ego and pride can keep us locked in the hallway for years, but we can come out at any time. This book is some of what I learned, and I hope it will shorten *your* stay in the hallway.

The Hell of Resentment and Fear

If you find yourself in hell, keep moving.

When someone hurts me, I know that forgiveness is cheaper than a lawsuit, but not nearly as gratifying.

My addictions are like the skins of an onion. In retrospect, giving up alcohol was easy when compared to giving up compulsive spending, or Big Deal chasing, or the behavior that gets me into a situation where I want to be rescued or bailed out.

Keep a journal. If you're angry and don't know why, write it down. Resist the temptation to judge what you've written.

Attack the shark that's swimming closest.

How do I know I'm an addict? I won't open a box of cookies, but if it's open, I'll eat the whole box. Same goes for Ben & Jerry's.

It is said that to find inner peace, we need to finish all things we have started. So I looked around my house to see things I had started and hadn't finished. Before leaving the house, I had finished off a bottle of merlot, a bottle of chardonnay, a bottle of Baileys, a bottle of Kahlúa, a package of Oreos, a pot of coffee, the rest of the cheesecake, some saltines, and a box of Godiva chocolates.

You can't hear anything when you're yelling.

Unless you recognize where you went wrong, you don't stand a chance of eliminating that pattern of behavior from your life.

I find accidents happen to me when I'm not in my body.

Alcoholics are extreme.

If you decide you're going to lose, even a loser can beat you.

Do not spend one more day in agony, for it increases the agony of the world.

I have a black belt in pain-aversion therapy.

Nothing sharpens one's mind more than a trip to the gallows.

My perfectionism will kill me in my recovery.

How much time do we spend during the day on fear, regret, and sorrow? Well, that's how we frame the day and create our experience.

When we alcoholics are upset, we will do anything to erase the discomfort of the feeling. But what we really need to do is nothing. Sitting with the discomfort is the hardest and the most necessary thing to do.

Fear is a soul sickness in its own right.

A friendship that can't handle a little nervous breakdown is not a friendship at all.

The danger of negative self-talk is that we look for evidence to make it true.

We hold on to suffering because if we let go of it, then what?

When the pain of living with an addiction becomes greater than our fear of changing, we are ready to change.

The more you love somebody who is a suffering addict, the harder it is just to love them and do nothing.

It takes years to build up trust, and only seconds to destroy it.

You shouldn't be so eager to find out a secret. It could change your life forever.

Self-pity is about not getting what we want.

Who are you punishing when you hate someone?

People want to hear you complain about as much as you want to hear them.

Sometimes when I'm angry, I have the right to be angry, but that doesn't give me the right to be cruel.

It's a lot easier to react than it is to think.

You can do something in an instant that will give you a heartache for life.

Two men in a burning house must not stop to argue.
—CHINESE PROVERB

To fear death is to misunderstand life.

I don't attract lunatics; I demand them.

Having a strong tolerance for crazy and participating in it are two different things.

Stop blaming.

Suffering is a choice.

Never react out of anger, hurt feelings, or envy. You will always regret it.

If I am buried in self-pity, I can't be of service to anybody, least of all to myself.

All emotional pain is ego, the bruised ego.

11

The people who are the easiest to hate are the ones who need our love the most.

Healing from addiction is like childbirth. The contractions get more frequent and the pain more intense, but it is in the very contractions themselves that God gives us the lesson.

If you catch yourself regretting things you said or didn't say, release those regrets. This is addictive thinking.

Let go of toxic people, places, and things.

Be wary of giving advice. To many people, it feels like criticism.

Whatever anger you don't release becomes internalized and sabotages your health.

Selfishness and self-centeredness are the root of all our trouble.

Say what you mean, mean what you say, but don't say it mean!

You can only light your cigarette once by sticking your head in the oven.

Have zero tolerance today for thoughts of regret, fear, and sorrow. If you have such thoughts, observe them without judgment and say, "I'm only human."

All addiction is progressive. Any addiction, if untreated, results in a downward spiral and is ultimately fatal.

"Faith: Firm belief in something for which there is no proof."
—*MERRIAM-WEBSTER'S COLLEGIATE DICTIONARY*

When you care so much about what people think of you, you become a cheap mirror image reflecting others' lives.

Things can go from the very worst to the very best within a blink of an eye.

People know when you don't like them.

"He who sets himself up as a judge of truth and knowledge is shipwrecked by the laughter of the Gods."
—ALBERT EINSTEIN

"The wise man in the storm prays to God not for safety from danger, but deliverance from fear."
—RALPH WALDO EMERSON

Discomfort is the gateway to a new perception.

Never interrupt. Trust me, people just hate it.

Failure is not falling down. It is refusing to get back up.

Some hearts are so hard that God can only enter by breaking them.

Alcoholic Alzheimer's: Forgetting everything but the grudges.

Not drinking without a program is like being in a speeding car without a steering wheel.

You must pay particular attention not to those who laugh, but to those who don't.

Why should I waste my time reliving the past when I can spend it worrying about the future?

Today I will gladly share my experience and advice, for there are no sweeter words than "I told you so!"

I need not suffer in silence while I can still moan, whimper, and complain.

I am grateful that I am not as judgmental as all those censorious, self-righteous people around me.

Fear and rage are two emotions frequently responsible for heart attacks.

When men drink, they get drunk. When women drink, they get tipsy.

GUILT: God Understands I Lack Trust.

At any given moment, we are either responding from love or reacting from fear.

Guilt is the reverse side of the coin of pride.

FEAR: False Evidence Appearing Real.

If you cannot love yourself, you cannot love others and you cannot stand to see others loved.

Fear grows in the dark. If we think there is a bogeyman around the corner, turn on the light.

I suffer from wanting to decorate the cake when there *is* no cake.

The point you suffer through is not fun, but it's where the gold is.

In life, that which you can't control controls you.

Stop arguing with the world. You're going to lose.

Depression is anger turned inward.

There are only two sins: The first is to interfere with the growth of another human being. The second is to interfere with one's own growth.

You affirm what you constantly think about.

Most of our psychological problems are really just rotten choices.

If you can't control your emotional state, you must be addicted to it.

The lie stops you from confronting the truth.

Go toward the thing you hate the most.

Debting is an addiction to deprivation.

Success is going toward the thing that scares you and doing it anyway.

Gambling is an addiction to losing.

Experience is what happens when life doesn't work out the way we want. It's how we learn.

Don't let a dispute injure a great relationship.

You used to have to scrape me off to get rid of me.

You cannot open a flower with a sledgehammer.

Shame assumes the other person knows something you don't.

I am fearful of what I think is reality.

Complacency is the worst sin.

Whose life are you making easy?

Every artist is, at some point, a laborer.

What's the worst thing that could happen? Sometimes when we are afraid to look at this, our vagueness creates a far worse outcome.

If you move to take the fear away, you'll never get to the root of the problem.

Ask two questions about fear: Why am I afraid? Is it true?

Do you ever wake up in the middle of the night and the Fear Express is running right through your bedroom?

At any given moment, there are 1,500 words of negative self-talk telling you that you can't do something.

No unhappiness is too great to be lessened.

When I was drinking, my soul was dying. It was like a pea rolling around in a box.

Disagreements with loved ones are only about the present situation. Don't bring in the past.

If you don't look at yourself and take stock, you will always live in the past.

If you are uncomfortable, you may be experiencing one of the seven deadly sins, or the PAGGLES: pride, anger, greed, gluttony, lust, envy, or sloth.

As long as we are looking in the mirror at ourselves, it's not going to be very interesting.

"The artist is nothing without the gift, but the gift is nothing without work."
—ÉMILE ZOLA

The definition of an addiction is really simple: It's something you can't stop.

Fear is a four-letter word.

Stop judging.

I don't have to tell everybody everything. I only do it because I want them to like me, but it invariably backfires.

If it's detestable to you, don't do it to someone else.

Holding on to blame, guilt, anger, and resentment is the greatest killer known to humanity.

You—not your past—are responsible for your resentments.

If you were oppressed and abused as a child, you may internalize the oppressor and actually become him or her in your life today.

Criticism is an adult form of a childhood cry.

Allow what you fear to question what you cherish.

I was addicted to excited misery.

Never do anything to harm anyone.

If you don't have a plan, your plan can't fail.

Three reasons why we are unhappy:
1. We get used to what we have, and we want more.
2. We don't stop to realize that we have good health.
3. A painful event eradicates everything else, and we forget our blessings.

I can feel so close to God when I'm in the hallway of fear, but when things are going great, it's "God who?"

Depression is loss.

I'm guilty of sabotaging myself so I can get saved.

The fear of what *might* happen is usually something that has already happened.

Fear is the absence of light.

If you remove the resentment, what is left is pure love.

The memory of your first high is encoded in your brain. The life of addiction is spent chasing down that first high.

Chances are, if there's an obstacle in your life, it's you.

In order to move ahead, you must have brutal honesty about where you are.

Get rid of all vampire people in your life.

We can be dragged down to nothingness by our fears.

If God drives, what's to fear?

We have to solve the problem we've been given, not the one we want.

Every river is stuck in its bed.

You're ruined by how easy life is for you.

You need to be alone in your affliction to get to your essence.

Do what's hardest to do—the thing you don't want to do—otherwise it will haunt you.

If you want them to stop their addiction, pray for their bottom to be raised.

To be free of a resentment, pray for people every day for two weeks. Pray that they get everything their heart desires, even if you don't mean it.

Discomfort is the key to identifying the problem.

Everyone has to learn to manage fear.

Don't let the bastards beat you down.

When you say, "I want," that's what you get: *want*.

I was a gifted drinker.

If you don't think money is a mood-altering substance, just put $500 in your pocket and see what happens.

When you're unhappy with your behavior in certain situations, ask yourself, "What's this behavior doing for me?"

If you don't have anything better to offer than silence, keep your words to yourself.

Expectations are premeditated resentments.

Be careful of any stick you pick up; there's always another end you can't see.

Know your enemy, talk to your enemy, don't feature your enemy.

Does it need to be said? Does is need to be said now? Does it need to be said by me?

Trying to please people and relying on them for financial security keeps you living in fear.

Reasons we fail: negative self-talk, poor self-image, and need for approval.

Your mind is like a bad neighborhood. You should never go in there alone.

If you're afraid, people will respond to the fear and that's what they will remember about you.

Negative thoughts are as bad as negative actions.

If you're going to be bad, be bad and loud.

We hold on to resentments because deep down we realize once they are gone, we will have to deal with the pain.

I grow at the speed of pain.

The fastest way to end an argument is to give up being right.

The Fruits of Faith:
Forgiveness, Courage, and Grace

Risk being great.

The act of letting go is practicing faith.

A gift is something voluntarily given from one person to another without compensation, or a special favor from God. Sobriety is a gift.

I am more than enough.

When there is nothing left but God, you find out that God is all you need.

Create a joy list. Make a list of all your blessings, including people, events, and praiseworthy things about yourself. Read it at the end of each week.

All perfection and all virtues of the Deity are hidden inside you—reveal them.

Love and serve all humanity. Assist everyone.

If we have faith, God will open a door for us—not necessarily the door we would have chosen, but the right one nevertheless.

In the exact moment of my last drink, I was given a nanosecond of grace.

The ABCs of aging: Accept, Bloom late, Celebrate, Dance at weddings, Enjoy the small things, Fall in love again, Gratitude, Hold hands, Inspire, Jettison grudges, Knowledge, Laugh, Mend fences, Nurture friendships, Open your heart, Play the harmonica, Question, Resiliency, Smile, Teach someone to read, Understand, Volunteer, Wonder, become an "X" something, Yodel, Zest.

What comes from the heart goes to the heart.

On Thanksgiving, ask each person around the table to give thanks for one thing.

All God requires of me is that I be kind, generous, and loving. When I'm not, he gives me a little nudge to remind me.

A friend who was fifty years sober was asked about how he maintained such long-term sobriety. He said, "Don't drink and don't die."

An apology can heal a lifetime of pain in an instant.

It's what you see—not what you think you see—that matters.

"The deepest level of communication is not communication, but communion. It is wordless. It is beyond words, and it is beyond speech, and it is beyond concept. Not that we discover a new unity. We discover an older unity. My dear brothers, we are already one. But we imagine that we are not. What we have to recover is our original unity. What we have to be is what we are."
—THOMAS MERTON

Feeling your rage is the beginning of forgiveness.

Have you ever stopped and looked at yourself through the eyes of the Ultimate Observer?

God limits the obstacles he gives us because they could destroy us.

Life is a series of turning corners.

What thing did I do today to fulfill my vision?

Pray for the willingness to forgive.

The miracle of my last drink and of every alcoholic's last drink is nothing short of a moment of divine grace. One moment you're a hopeless drunk, and the next moment you are a hope-filled child of God.

THE FRUITS OF FAITH

You bow with your knees, not with your feelings.

You've got to give yourself permission.

Is it doable?

Watch your behavior when no one is looking.

Joy is wholehearted acceptance.

Ego: The layers we place between ourselves and God.

"Lord, take me where you want me to go
Let me meet who you want me to meet
Tell me what you want me to say and
Keep me out of your way."
—FATHER MYCHAL F. JUDGE, O.F.M., CHAPLAIN, FIRE DEPARTMENT—
CITY OF NEW YORK, KILLED IN THE SEPTEMBER 11, 2001, ATTACK ON
THE WORLD TRADE CENTER

Prayer is service of the heart.

If you don't like the way the world is run, complain to the management: your Higher Power.

Tears happen. Endure, grieve, and move on.

Great love and great achievements involve great risk.

If you remember God is walking beside you at all times, you will never experience doubt or fear.

Be the kind of person you want to attract.

We must act as if all the right people are present.

Choose company in whose presence you are elevated.

What makes us human:
- ability to be ashamed
- ability to be kind
- ability to be merciful

Sometimes we think we're going somewhere for a particular reason, but our Higher Spirit is really sending us there for another purpose.

Invite God into your relationship.

When you have something that you know is right, adjust everything to suit it.

In God's time, not ours.

As soon as you move the idea into reality, the idea starts to change.

If you have the truth, you can talk to the whole world.

What humanity can conceive, God can achieve.

When you're spiritually awake, you open yourself to dreaming.

Retrace your steps up to the inspiration.

A spiritual journey: The self leaves the place that shaped the self in order to transform the self.

God is in the silence. Embrace his soundless sound.

Sleep renews the soul.

Only with God in your life can you respect another person in your life, otherwise it's just self-love.

We are human beings, not human doings.

If your life isn't working, work with others.

One small turn in our lives can lead to great change and to open doors that we never anticipated. It is within all of us to repair the fragments, to reconnect with those we love on a deeper level.

If we are willing to let God lead, we can dance through each season of life.

Everything you do either connects you or disconnects you.

Think good and it will be good.

Atonement: At-one-ment with God.

When my son Grant was a baby, I'd yell, "God, Grant!" I realize now that I was partway through the Serenity Prayer.

I have no idea what God is, but I know there is a God.

I love you not because of who you are, but because of who I am when I'm with you.

Do all you can to develop your faith in God.

If you don't need approval from anyone, then you will be free to be your authentic self.

Pray with an attentive heart, and all the doors of heaven will open to you.

Depression is spiritual self-mutilation.

Thank God for not giving you what you want.

It's easier to pray when you're happy. It's very hard to pray when you're depressed, which is when you need it the most. Depression is about ego, and praying is about humility.

The moment of clarity or grace or getting honest is called a "bottom." There is nothing that can accelerate this journey except your individual capacity for pain.

Recovery is not for wusses. You must have faith and courage and ask for help. Others have done it and recovered. Use their examples for inspiration and hope.

Every year on September 10, I send this e-mail: Just for today, September 10, rejoice in the ordinary. Revel in the boredom, countless irritations, and disappointments. Be grateful for the missed bus, waiting on hold, the line at the post office. Forgive the one person you can't. And above all, tell someone—who you're positive knows it already—that you love them.

Learn to be grateful in the moment just before the storm.

When people are in need, we must be God to them.

Because of God's grace, failure is not final.

The fruits of the spirit are love, faithfulness, goodness, patience, kindness, peace, humility, joy, and self-control.

"What does the Lord require of you but to do justice, and to love kindness, and to walk humbly with your God?"
—MICAH 6:8

Dear God, help me. Send me a sign so I know you're listening.

Elisabeth Kübler-Ross's five stages of death and dying apply to any loss: denial and isolation, anger, bargaining, depression, acceptance.

Seek the sacred within the ordinary.

Heroes are the people who do what has to be done when it needs to be done, regardless of the consequences.

You only go in two directions: toward God or away from God.

It is the human mind that questions God's plan for us. For it is by taking away that God makes room for the divine in our lives. It is only our arrogance that questions. This is where faith is born.

Go do good.

Life always gives you a second chance.

Praying is like a conversation in a marriage or with a best friend. Begin a companionship with God, acknowledging all your hopes and dreams. Then listen.

Do what you were created to do, and you will find the power of your own "godliness."

Every morning pray for "Courage." It is a one-word prayer.

I believe that God has brought me to the precipice—not to have me jump in but to have me leap over.

Do not be afraid. You are not alone.

We are not separate. We are all connected.

If we feel we are worthy and deserving, it just flows.

Every moment of the day is an opportunity for healing.

Sometimes we have to let go of the person in the dream, but keep the dream.

What do you do when something happens to challenge your joy?

I'm willing to let go of being the problem.

Everything has its way out.

Our background and circumstances may have influenced who we are, but we are responsible for who we become.

Hope is our best currency when we have lost everything.

To be with people who are dying gives more to me than it does to them.

If we passionately believe in what does not exist, we will create its existence.

I can't afford the luxury of a negative thought.

Sometimes I fear that if I lose interest in myself, I will disappear.

Even when performing charity, justice, and "walking with the Lord," do it modestly.

Have faith, and all the right people will show up to help you.

When the spirit inside us connects to our Higher Spirit, it opens a channel of healing energy.

Forgiveness is a gift we give to ourselves.

If someone calls you, just remember they are supposed to. God is screening your calls.

If you plant a tree, you don't pick it up every day to see how it's growing.

"True religion is the life we lead, not the creed we profess."
—LOUIS NIZER

May all your prayers be answered.

A man in a bar in Alaska was debating the existence of God. He told a friend how he was lost in the wilderness, and how he prayed for God to save him—if there was a God.

"Well," said the friend, "I guess there must be a God, because you are here now."

The man replied, "Oh no. The Inuit came and got me."

Darkness: When God appears to have hidden his face.

Recovery is in the details.

The secrets to happiness in life are acceptance and forgiveness.

The word *ritual* is in the word *spiritual*.

Pain is the touchstone of growth.

God removes his presence from us in order to renew our faith.

Pain is calling me home to God.

What would God do in a situation like this?

We come to this earth either to learn or to teach a lesson. When we are finished, our purpose here is complete.

For suffering to have a purpose, we must have pain with understanding.

The only person who is with you your entire life is yourself.

The Torah summed up in one sentence: Love your friends as you love yourself.

With faith, anything is possible.

Don't put more in the vessel than the vessel can hold.

The perfect solution starts in the spiritual realm. Thoughts become words and create a state of being, doing, and acting.

Be alive while you are alive.

Think about what you want to give rather than what you want to get.

The helping hand that I was looking for my entire life was attached to my arm.

If you feel God's absence, who moved?

How do you want to leave the world?

You can't get sober alone.

Don't ever work or live higher than a firefighter's ladder.

Buddhists believe we are born with a certain number of breaths before we die. Jews believe we are born with a certain number of words.

The battle is not yours, it's God's.

To solve the problems of life is neither to multiply the quantity nor to escape, it is to search for the causes. Once you find the cause, the problem is half solved.

Want more for others than you want for yourself.

Where's God? Wherever you let him in.

God moves in mysterious ways. Be brave enough to open your heart.

A daily prayer: God bless all my friends, providing what they need this day! And may their lives be full of your peace, prosperity, and power as they seek to have a closer relationship with you.

"The fruit of silence is prayer
The fruit of prayer is faith
The fruit of faith is love
The fruit of love is service
The fruit of service is peace."

—MOTHER TERESA

I am willing to be relieved of the need to be unworthy.

The essence of communication is love.

Our willingness and God's grace coincide when we get sober.

Your real work is to grow spiritually. Any economic gains are to assist in that end.

Create what you want to happen.

A prayer: I believe I'm divinely guided. I believe I will take the right road. When there is no road, God will help me find the road.

Every time you don't act on your addictions is an act of self-love.

Until I had completely lost everything, I could not completely have anything.

Embrace the adversity. It always contains a pearl of a gift.

Focus on the possibility of miracles happening when you least expect them.

Michelangelo created the statue of David by chipping away everything that was not David.

Thank God for every success and every disappointment. Thank him more for the disappointments because they are how you learn.

Visualize your door, and walk through it.

Focus your dreams, write them down, and ask for them. Be specific and say them out loud.

Spiritual recovery: The more you give, the more you gain.

Strive to be your authentic self.

If God brings you to it, he will bring you through it.

Look forward to the next morning.

The sweet things of life are the little moments strung together that teach us how to love and be loved.

Sometimes the best action is to do nothing.

Rejection is God's protection.

Never gossip.

Say "yes" to everything for two weeks, and look for how to get to "yes" in every situation.

Say "no" to good, "yes" to great.

Go into the day with poise, delicacy, and grace.

Listen to your intuition. Those quiet inner voices contain spiritual messages.

The Joy of Coincidence and Serendipity

Begin a thing. It will rarely end up where you thought it would. Start it and let it tell *you* what it wants to be.

Everything is waiting to teach you.

Fill your life with joy and satisfaction.

I love people's sobriety stories. My favorite part is always the moment of their last drink or drug.

"When you realize how perfect it is, you will tilt your head back and laugh at the sky."

—BUDDHA

Whenever we encounter difficulties that change the course of our lives, we encounter God.

Believe in love at first sight.

Love deeply and passionately. You might get hurt, but it's the only way to live life completely.

Listen is an action verb.

Expect miracles. Miracles are the natural order of life. If we have the willingness to anticipate miracles, they have the potential to occur.

Most people are afraid to start something because they cannot envision the end of it. Just begin it. You will never finish it unless you begin it.

Be aware that all are one, equal but not the same.

Your choice creates the next moment.

Once we surrender our mind to God completely, he will take care of us in every way.

Faith is not belief without truth, but trust without reservation.

If we accept tough jobs as a challenge to our abilities, and wade through them with enthusiasm, miracles will happen.

Listen to the people who cheer you on rather than the ones who echo your fears.

Live expectantly. Expect better things, right up to the end of your life and beyond that.

Trust the universe.

Practice radical optimism.

Each important thing in life relating to love and work has been preceded by a huge coincidence.

When you awake, there is no reason why today can't be the best day of your life.

Listening requires you keep your big mouth shut.

Each day, look at things you take for granted, like food and trees. Be grateful. Can you actually sustain this gratitude for two minutes?

If you don't make a wish, it can't come true.

An attitude of crisis blocks you from recognizing spiritual coincidences that are happening all the time.

The artist's contribution is not what he thinks, but what he sees.

The world changes when the observer changes.

At any given moment, we have the choice to be the least we can be—or the most.

When you walk into a room, the place is talking to you. Do your best to listen.

The artist must be in complete awe of life.

Listening is the greatest gift you can give someone.

Hitting bottom is where the gold is, the true alchemy.

You have a chance to change every single day.

Surround yourself with what you love, whether it's family, friends, pets, keepsakes, music, plants, hobbies. Your home is your refuge.

When you do good, you bring forth angels.

Do one anonymous act of kindness a day and see how it makes you feel.

Only a person who's really awake can dream.

The good you do remains in the world forever.

If you don't take the leap, you will never know what it's like to fly.

Every person is a note in the cosmic symphony.

Follow the steps and actions of other people, not their words.

Coincidences are God's street signs telling us we're on the right path.

The next phone call or e-mail could change your life. If we go through the day with this anticipation, it is thrilling.

God breaks his anonymity when a coincidence occurs.

On Chinese New Year, you are supposed to wear red and only talk about being prosperous in the new year. Why can't we try that every day?

You can take a thimble or a bucket to the ocean; it makes no difference to the ocean.

Our most creative thoughts or inspirations come in a flash of intuition.

To the world, you may be one person, but to one person, you may be the world.

If you ask God, "What do I do now?" you'll never hear the answer if you don't shut up.

If your own house is in order, the answers will come.

"I did not come upon the theory of the creation of the Universe by the use of my rational mind."
—ALBERT EINSTEIN

Miracles happen when we start taking coincidences seriously.

Don't try so hard. The best things come when you least expect them.

Our thoughts create our reality.

Life is not measured by the number of breaths we take, but by the number of moments that take our breath away.

"Be the change you want to see in the world."
—GANDHI

I pray every morning to be relieved of the bondage of self, and God sends me a coincidence to let me know he's listening.

"It is the familiar that usually evades us in life. What is before our nose is what we see last."
—WILLIAM BARRETT

The miracle is not to fly in the air or to walk on the water but to walk on the earth.

Coincidences are messages propelling us toward our destiny.

Coincidences seem to cluster around important events or people in our lives, leading us to what we need to learn.

How Opportunity Happens:
Being Open to Life's Lessons, Overcoming Adversity, and Taking Action

The universe does not judge. People do.

The reward of sobriety is sobriety.

It takes more energy to wallow in self-pity than to take one positive action to help another.

If you listen, you learn. If you talk, you never learn.

The person who needs to learn the lesson of trust will experience the distrust of others. An angry person will experience anger from others. Life is a mirror.

All things don't have the same value.

In order to make permanent changes, you must be willing to see things differently.

Don't complain for two weeks. If you do, start over.

Put a rubber band around your wrist. Every time you have a negative thought, replace it with a positive thought and *snap out of it!*

We must choose that quality that is against our nature. That quality is patience.

Your life doesn't work to the extent to which you break your agreements.

Listening is giving others their sacred space.

Cherish your health. If it is good, preserve it. If it could be better, improve it. If it is beyond what you can improve, get help.

I have a disconnect between myself and my experience.

If you have a disappointment, ask yourself immediately, "What did I learn?"

Make choices that expand your life, not diminish it.

Growth is not based on comfort.

You polish it here and it shines over there.

If you won't leave the room a better place, then you won't leave the world a better place.

Act. Don't react.

The last minute of your life is the most important. It is the sum of who you are.

Growing up is learning to exclude things gracefully.

If you're not moving forward, you're standing still.

There are two tragedies in this world: not getting what you want, and getting what you want.

Be yourself. Know yourself.

Tolerate the discomfort or you will never learn the lesson.

The solution to all problems: awareness, acceptance, action.

Begin it now.

It's important to know not where you are going, but what you are leaving behind.

In order to grow when things are going well, get out of your comfort zone.

Change your wristwatch to your nondominant hand.

Make no assumptions.

What action can I take today to make my dreams real? Get out of my own way.

Really listen to people when they are talking. Ask yourself, "Am I really listening, or am I thinking about what I'm going to say?"

The four freedoms of Franklin Delano Roosevelt:
1. Freedom from want.
2. Freedom of speech and expression.
3. Freedom of every person to worship God in his own way.
4. Freedom from fear, that no nation shall commit an act of physical aggression against any neighbor, anywhere in the world.

If you have negative thoughts about failing, imagine how a computer word-processing program works: "highlight" and "delete." And don't forget to empty the trash.

At the moment of commitment, the universe conspires to assist you.

When you feel doubt, agitation, or indecision, it's time to pause, relax, and take it easy.

Floss.

Everything is necessary, even our suffering and pain.

Action is the magic word. The only way to solve a problem is with action.

Do better today what you did yesterday.

When you're having a problem, disagreement, or altercation, make a list with four columns:
1. Write down the problem.
2. Write down who and what it involves.
3. Write down how it makes you feel (angry, sad, ashamed, and so on).
4. Write down your part in the conflict.

Nothing you ever give is lost, and everything you give is multiplied.

"Act your way into understanding. Be yourself. Everyone else is already taken."
—OSCAR WILDE

In recovery, we must lower our expectations.

"I have never been hurt by anything I didn't say."
—CALVIN COOLIDGE

My problem is that I hang on to a relationship way past the expiration date.

Don't just do something, stand there.

The only thing wrong with being the center of the universe is that it's so crowded.

Drop blaming from your speech and thought.

We are either the spider, the fly, or the web in between.

A good friend is better than a therapist.

All recovery is awareness, acceptance, action. When we are in pain, it is the awareness phase.

No matter how badly your heart is broken, the world doesn't stop for your grief.

If you want to hide something from an alcoholic, put it in a Bible. If you don't want to forget something, stick it in your underwear drawer.

We are responsible for what we do, no matter how we feel.

Always leave loved ones with loving words. It may be the last time you see them.

You never step in the same river twice.

My mind hears what my mouth is saying.

Give people more than they expect, and do it cheerfully.

Ideas are like spaghetti. You have to keep throwing them against the wall to see if anything sticks.

Sometimes it's not about me.

Three words to strike from your vocabulary: *coulda, shoulda, woulda*.

Every word you speak generates energy, so be careful.

We can find happiness no matter what somebody else is doing.

Whatever you think becomes real. The thought precedes the reality.

I always have to check: is this real thinking or is this magical thinking?

Be grateful for the cheerleaders in your life. Fans are the most valuable kinds of friends to have.

In order for us to change, we must completely change our belief systems about ourselves.

If you want to know what needs to be healed, ask yourself where it hurts the most.

If you believe that you can harm, then you can also heal.

When I act on my addictions, I actually get a physical feeling of nausea at the back of my throat. All the feelings of self-loathing and shame that accompanied my drinking are present.

Thoughts become words. Words become actions. Actions become habits. Habits become character. Character becomes your destiny.

If you want to change, risk the unfamiliar. Change is characteristic of all growth.

Dare, dare, and then dare more.

Always take the high road. It's a lot less crowded.

Praise every soul. If you cannot praise someone, let them pass out of your life.

When you change the way you look at things, the things you look at change.

We are given obstacles to test us and renew our free will.

The greater you become, the greater your tests.

"When in doubt . . . don't."
—MY MOTHER

Sit with the discomfort. That is where the healing is.

Take an appropriate action and turn over the results.

The importance of the lesson is directly proportional to the amount of pain you're in.

Think before you speak. Don't say the first thing that comes into your mind. Instead, say the second.

Write down all the bad things in your past on a piece of paper and burn it. When you do this, be willing to release the past. When conflicts arise on a daily basis, write them down and burn them.

The measure of your progress is the enormity of the test.

The deeper you surrender to a thing, the more it will influence you.

In the point of view you disagree with, you must find the parts you agree with.

Change is doing.

Be on time.

The 3 Rs:
- respect for self
- respect for others
- responsibility for all your actions

When you're wrong, promptly admit it.

Life is not a casual place.

The learning is in the doing.

Only great minds explore the obvious.

Your body is smarter than your brain. Your body will have an idea before your stupid brain does. Listen to your body.

More important than making it better is making it happen.

In the greatest tragedies of our life comes the greatest light.

Get rid of the words *always* and *never.*

Share your knowledge. It's a way to achieve immortality.

To create what you want, you need to take action in the present moment. Tomorrow never comes.

Everything is for the best.

The great relationship is when your love for each other exceeds your need for each other.

Once a year, do something you've never done before.

Never break your word.

Difficulties are challenges sent to repair our selves.

"Life is not a choice. Your choice is your talent."
—STELLA ADLER

The Conflict Zone:
Money, Work, and Family

I have a friend who charges $1,000 an hour as a consultant: $200 for the work and $800 for his clients to take him seriously.

My job was getting over on people.

If we are wounded by our parents, we will seek them out unconsciously to repair the relationship. It should be no mystery why we keep winding up with the same lovers and bosses.

Why don't you invite God into your financial program?

I used to think that I was "only" an alcoholic, but when I put down the drink, I picked up credit cards. I realized debting was just as insidious. I would actually go into a blackout with an American Express card in my hand.

Our relationships are spiritual messengers.

Abstinence is the first tool to use to get out of debt. Credit is like booze to the drunk. I was a blackout drinker; why should I be any different with a credit card?

Every drawing my son does is a Picasso. I learned this because my childhood efforts were not admired; they were even criticized.

Here's the money song (just make up any ol' tune). Don't laugh, just sing it. It works, and at the very least, you're not worrying about money when you're singing it:

> Money, money, money flying in my windows.
> Money, money, money flying in my doors.
> Money, money, money coming in my mailbox.
> Ain't gonna worry 'bout money no more.

When you get a divorce, you have to go through a whole year of birthdays, anniversaries, and holidays before you can begin to heal.

I knew it was time to get a divorce when my family members were watching the same television channel in three different rooms.

You can get by on charm for about fifteen minutes. After that, you'd better know something.

Regardless of your relationship with your parents, you miss them terribly after they die.

I thought I had lost everything, but then I lost even more.

The secret to happiness: gratitude, acceptance, forgiveness.

You don't meet anyone while sitting in your apartment.

You have to kiss a lot of frogs so you will recognize the prince.

People will forget what you said, people will forget what you did, but people will never forget how you made them feel.

We are ruled by the people we hated in high school.

When choosing a mate, make a list:
1. List all the qualities and characteristics you want in a mate.
2. List all the things you don't want.
3. List things you'll put up with.
This way, you will recognize him or her when you meet.

The greatest way to teach our children is by example. Don't tell them how to behave. Show them.

When our children see our ability to forgive and accept ourselves, they adopt the same capabilities.

When our children misbehave, ask them, "What would you do if you were the parent?" Then make an agreement as to what the appropriate action is.

Let your children see your wisdom. They will remember it.

A child can sense our guilt.

We cannot create another person's reality.

If your children see your ability to forgive, they will know your true love for them.

All you can do is be someone who can be loved. The rest is up to others.

When your child walks into the room, all he or she wants to see is whether your eyes light up.

When dealing with misbehaving children, tell them that you love them and that it is not them but their behavior you don't approve of.

Recognize that you are not bad, but sometimes your behavior is bad.

You are enough today. You have enough today.

We don't have to change friends if we understand that friends change.

Just because two people argue, it doesn't mean they don't love each other.

Try not to take everything so damned personally.

Showing up for your friends and family is the greatest gift you can give.

The best part of a long-term friendship is the shorthand you have with each other.

In times of profound change, the learners inherit the earth. Meanwhile, the learned find themselves beautifully equipped to deal with a world that no longer exists.

Listen to those little voices, because they will change your life. You must listen carefully, because they often whisper.

You know you're over a former lover if you delete his or her phone messages.

The most valuable lessons of my marriage came after the divorce.

Never tell a child that dreams are unlikely or outlandish. Few things are more humiliating, and what a tragedy it would be if the child believed it.

There are people who love you dearly but just don't know how to show it.

Either you control your attitude or it controls you.

When you say "I love you," mean it.

Don't say that you love people unless you are willing to put them first.

When you say "I'm sorry," look the person in the eye.

Marry a person you love to talk to. As you get older, his or her conversational skills will be as important as any other quality.

My relationship with my teenage son was transformed when I stopped blaming and judging him and just loved him unconditionally.

Pray to be solvent one day at a time, and give thanks for abundance and health.

When we have a smothering parent, chances are we will become fiercely independent.

If you feel like acting out through shopping, eating, or drinking, ask yourself what you are afraid of in that moment.

When you are grappling with a life decision, put it on the shelf without judgment. The answer will come in time.

Our ability to forgive is the measure of our success in our relationships.

A job is a place where they pay you money to do a service, nothing more.

Addiction is always about trying to change our mood and avoid life problems.

The hardest lesson of parenting is the paradox. You must love your children and let them go at the same time. You must trust that they have their own Higher Power, and it's not you.

Pain in marriage is usually related to some pain in childhood.

I no longer need to punish, deceive, or compromise myself, unless of course I want to stay employed.

Having control over myself is almost as good as having control over others.

If I had worked as hard on my marriage as I did on my divorce, we would probably be happily married today.

Thank your partner for being difficult. A partner's challenges are the key to your personal growth, if you have the courage.

It is possible to hate people at this very moment and still love them. This duality of relationships is the most difficult to live with.

"I bless my poverty, because it makes me paint the bread as if I could eat it."
                                        —VINCENT VAN GOGH

If you live long enough, you get to lose everything.

Think about these things. You may not realize it, but all these statements are 100 percent true.

1. At least two people in this world love you so much they would die for you.
2. At least fifteen people in this world love you in some way.
3. A smile from you can bring happiness to anyone, even if they don't like you.
4. Every night, someone thinks about you before going to sleep.
5. You mean the world to someone.
6. If not for you, someone may not be living.
7. You are special and unique.
8. When you make the biggest mistake ever, something good can still come from it.
9. When you think the world has turned its back on you, take a look. You most likely turned your back on the world.
10. Someone you don't even know exists loves you.
11. Always remember the compliments you receive. Forget about the rude remarks.

12. Always tell people how you feel about them. You will feel much better when they know, and you'll both be happy.
13. If you have great friends, take the time to let them know that they are great.

If you want to figure out what to do in life, ask yourself what you would do if you didn't have to work.

Perfect an "elevator pitch" about who you are. You should be able to pitch yourself in twenty seconds.

Send no e-mails when you're mad.

Embrace the task at hand, and do it clearly and honestly.

When you are working with others, be sure to use the word *we* and not *I*. It's a small thing, but it means the world to the people you work with.

Want to lose ten pounds? Eat less. Move more.

Your children are citizens of a universe. They will encounter obstacles as well as fulfillments. Bestow upon your children the blessing of your faith. Give your children permission to make their own lives independent of you.

Wholeheartedly accept your children's human frailties as well as their abilities and virtues.

Give your children unconditional love, a love that is not dependent on report cards, clean hands, or popularity.

I didn't see my true gifts and talents until I stopped looking for them in others.

Create a space in yourself to make room for other people.

If you get into an unavoidable argument, the best way out is to say, "I'm sorry you feel that way. You may be right."

Practice detaching with love.

For actors, the formula is preparation, rehearsal, performance. This formula works for everything.

Work past mediocrity.

"Lay out your mission. Define the values to achieve that mission."
—JACK WELCH

When we lose our ego, the connection to others is immediate.

The family of an addict is like a mobile. Family members adjust their behavior to the dysfunction to balance the mobile.

Avoid people who make you feel bad about yourself. Chances are, you do a good enough job of making yourself feel bad.

Practice restraint of pen, tongue, and e-mail.

Be nice. Likability is more important than competency.

Write down five things you're passionate about.

Be unapologetically passionate about your art and your life.

We are mirrors of each other. If someone annoys you, you're probably reacting to a part of yourself that you don't like.

I want to take this opportunity to thank everyone who ever fired me, for it opened a door that was previously locked.

The things that attract you in the beginning of the relationship are the very things that repel you at the end.

What I fear in a relationship is becoming the "dining dead": those couples in the restaurants who don't talk to each other.

If you live in fear of not having money, you will never have it.

A relationship is something to be discovered, not defined by our expectations.

Remember this when talking to your children: the vessel only needs what it can hold.

People don't change. We have to change to meet them.

"If I'd gotten the job I wanted at Montgomery Ward, I suppose I would never have left Illinois."
　　　　　　　　—RONALD REAGAN

If we cannot love ourselves, we cannot love others.

If you are mistrustful, you will see mistrust in others.

If you want to be rich, you have to think like a rich person. What would a millionaire do in this situation? Donald Trump doesn't sit around thinking, "Where is the rent going to come from?"

How do I feel? What do I want? What are my reasonable expectations?

True love is not losing one's self in another's eyes. Rather, true love is two people looking out into the world with the same pair of eyes.

"The pain of unrequited love is rivaled only by the pain of love fulfilled."
—OSCAR WILDE

Don't waste your time on a man or woman who won't waste his or her time on you.

Invite God into your relationship with money.

Say yes to the Divine.

If you are "disabled" around money, preplan every purchase.

How to raise your children: encourage, encourage, encourage.

Writers write. Painters paint. Musicians make music. The rest of us have to learn it.

The perfect relationship: When a couple is able to hold on to a string and let go of it at the same time.

If you hate your job, use that energy to focus on your dreams.

All people fall into four categories: intimidators, interrogators, poor me, aloof drama. Once you know this, you can figure anyone out.

Just because someone doesn't love you the way you want them to, it doesn't mean they don't love you with all they have.

I am willing to stop spending money I don't have.

Until you're ready to have money, God won't give it to you.

What you do for others is always in your control.

Intimacy: In to me see.

Remember who signs your paycheck.

Don't ever say "I will not have money." Words are powerful.

Abundance is about the flow of energy.

"We convince others by our presence."
—WALT WHITMAN

Create an opening statement that opens doors.

Just shut up and listen!

At the end of the job say, "Thank you for the opportunity for me to be of service."

Never apologize for what you are selling.

Get an action partner.

Write down your goals on a calendar.

Write down your visions.

Smile when picking up the phone. The caller will hear it in your voice.

If you don't know where your money goes, write down every penny you spend and make a monthly spreadsheet of all your expenditures.

Make a spreadsheet of how you spend your time.

Consider the source.

Don't take anything personally. What people think of you is none of your business.

To find work, write down everyone and everything you know.

Write down your dreams with your nondominant hand.

To find work, write down everything you ever did for work.

To find work, be willing to do anything to work.

God is my employer. All work is service. Be of service to the cause of a better world.

Nurturing Resiliency:
The Springboard for Joy and Laughter

Remember in life, if you coast, you coast uphill.

When stating your vision, never say "I wish . . . ," "I want . . . ," "I hope . . ." Be emphatic. Say "I will . . ."

Do things in order.

"Willing: Done, borne, or accepted by choice or without reluctance."
—*MERRIAM-WEBSTER'S COLLEGIATE DICTIONARY*

Observing is fun. Doing is hard.

In India, there are laugh clinics along the river every morning.

Denial is a tool that often enables a person to survive intolerable situations and abuses. People deny to survive.

Freedom from disorder is a life that is beautiful.

If you are willing to face all of your creditors, most will be willing to meet you halfway. It's in their best interest to have you pay something rather than nothing.

A friend of mine knew Mother Teresa. She was bemoaning all of her daily problems, to which Mother Teresa replied with great exuberance, "Oh, God must love you so much to visit these trials upon you."

In recovery, we retire the Judge.

Drop *if only* from your vocabulary.

An alcoholic's prayer: Help me to be willing to accept your answer to my prayers, whether or not it is the answer that I thought I wanted. You know that I have trouble with acceptance sometimes, God, so there are times when you will need to help me be willing to be willing.

"My father gave me two things: he conceived me and pissed on my dreams."
—FRANK SINATRA

Write your autobiography, starting with your earliest memories. When you hit a story that makes you cringe, ask, "What did I do? Why did I do it? How did it make me feel?"

Every day you should reach out and touch someone.

It can feel safe to hide behind laughter, creating a noise over what we are not willing to look at. If we become willing to confront those issues that make us uncomfortable, laughter will become a gift rather than a mask.

"Creativity is contagious. Pass it on."
—ALBERT EINSTEIN

"Once you can accept the universe as being something expanding into an infinite nothing which is something . . . wearing stripes with plaid is easy."
—ALBERT EINSTEIN

I had to lose everything to find out how much I really had.

I used to think that I completely reinvented myself at sixty-two, but then it occurred to me, God had completely reinvented me.

Vulnerability is the only place of real change.

Nobody can "do you" but you.

Laughter brings us closer to the *yes*.

People love a warm hug or just a friendly pat on the back.

Have no lower expectation than illumination.

If you do not think before you speak, your good circumstances will disappear and your bad circumstances will increase.

A person without a sense of humor is like a wagon without springs—jolted by every pebble.

"You're always trying to get things to come out perfect in art 'cause it's a little bit different in life."
                                        —*ANNIE HALL*

If you live in the past and regret the past, it keeps you in the past.

You have to do anything twenty-one times to make it a habit.

A gem is not polished without rubbing, nor is a man made perfect without trials.

The Blackmail Diet really works. Draw up a contract that you must lose a specific amount of weight by a certain time. If you don't lose the weight, you must donate a specific amount of money to your most reviled and hated cause.

When doing a personal inventory, write down your feelings about the following questions:

1. Looking back over your life, what memories do you have that are guilt-ridden, painful, or dirty?
2. Today, what makes you feel inadequate as a human being?
3. Whom do you resent? Make a chart of who it is, the event, and how it threatens you emotionally.
4. What are your character defects, as you perceive them? Here's where the seven deadly sins come in, or the PAGGLES: pride, anger, greed, gluttony, lust, envy, and sloth. Also a consider a few extra goodies, such as despair, self-seeking, impatience, criticizing, jealousy, procrastination, laziness, negative thinking, self-justification, resentment, comparisons, selfishness, and ego.

5. What are the ongoing problems in your relationships?
6. What are your distortions on certain primary instincts in society, such as sex, security, and so on?
7. What are your goals today?
8. Do you see any ways you can start toward those goals?
9. What are your personality assets? This is a hard one for some, but it's so important to think about. Your traits might include being humble, modest, honest, patient, loving, forgiving, compassionate, trusting, generous, prompt, optimistic. If you're in recovery, first on this list should be "I'm an addict."

Getting sober and getting old are not for sissies.

You can keep going long after you think you can't.

Sometimes the people you expect to kick you when you're down will be the ones to help you get back up.

It's not what happens to people that's important. It's what they do about it.

If you want to know what God has in mind, just look around.

If you have problems you don't know how to solve, write them down and put them in a God Box. Leave them there and look at them six months from now.

The highest form of self-respect is to admit your mistakes and make amends for them.

When we were kids, time seemed to crawl. We couldn't wait for our birthdays and Christmas. Then you hit fifty, and every fifteen minutes is time for breakfast.

I lost everything after I had been sober for sixteen years. God knew I wouldn't be able to handle it before then.

When I feel powerless over life's problems, I have to remember that I was once powerless over alcohol. When I asked for help, my life changed instantly.

It is pride that changes angels into devils, and it is humility that changes people into angels.

On the Jewish New Year, they say it is a clean slate. We can make all new mistakes in the coming year.

"I was born at absolutely the right time. And I'm going to die not a moment too soon. That's the story of me. It's about timing."
—KATHARINE HEPBURN

There is no saint without a past. There is no sinner without a future.

I have a hard time connecting my body and the thing that's attached to it . . . my head.

Right actions for the future are the best apologies for wrong ones in the past.

You can tell when you are healing because that is when the pain is most acute. The pain is the arrow coming out, not the arrow going in.

The learning is in the doing.

Remember, we are *all* trying to succeed all the time in life. This will teach you compassion.

The way you overcome your obstacles is a measure of your greatness.

Maybe God wants you to meet a few wrong people so when you meet the right one, you will know how to be grateful.

Don't set yourself up for buffoonery.

You'll never hear the answer if you don't shut up.

Do not be afraid. You are not alone.

You are what you teach.

When all is said and done and you forget the words, all you really need to do is show up.

Tell people you love them at every available opportunity.

Judge your success by what you had to give up in order to get it.

Learn the rules so you can know how to break them properly.

When you lose, don't lose the lesson.

Not getting what you want is sometimes an incredible stroke of luck.

It is harder to change what is good in us than what is bad.

Deal with life on life's terms.

My job is not to make it great, but to make it better.

You can't control others if you can't control yourself.

You cannot make commitments without humility.

There are always going to be people who hurt you. So keep on trusting . . . be more careful about who you trust next time.

When I had my last drink, I thought my life was going to be one long dentist appointment.

A child chooses happiness over being right.

Risk being great.

To learn an art, go to people who do the art, not those who talk about it.

To solve a problem, look to the world for the solution.

Australians say, "Good on you!" I like that.

It's not whether you're good today, but whether you are better.

When the obstacles are surmounted, new obstacles are given to us.

Power struggles are often unconscious attempts to heal childhood wounds.

You can choose to win or lose.

Live well, laugh often, and love with all your heart.

A drunk is in front of a judge. The judge says, "You've been brought here for drinking."

The drunk says, "Okay, let's get started."

If sobriety were easy, everybody would be sober.

Laughter transcends the negative and you become one with God.

We are exactly where we are supposed to be.

It's always too soon to quit.

The most treasured friends are the ones who tell you the truth in a nurturing and loving way.

I don't know how to succeed, but I do know how to fail: try to please everyone.

Trying to talk to an alcoholic is like trying to blow out a lightbulb.

Widen your horizons, get an ever greater circle of friends, and above all, create opportunities for usefulness every single day of your life.

Talk doesn't cook rice.
—CHINESE PROVERB

If you're a rock on top of the mountain, you have farther to fall than one in the middle.

We fail because we set unrealistic goals. We should, instead, start with small possible changes.

I struggle to live in the *gray* of life.

Wrinkles reveal that we have lived and we have tried.

The Buddhists say that when speaking to an audience, begin with a joke because it opens the third eye of listening.

We should not expect ourselves to be any more perfect than the weather.

We receive from the world what we give to the world.

A true friend is someone who reaches for your hand and touches your heart.

Keep only cheerful friends. The grouches pull you down.

Throw out all nonessential numbers, including height, weight, and age. Let your doctor worry about them.

"What you can do, or dream you can do, begin it;
Boldness has genius, power, and magic in it."
—JOHANN WOLFGANG VON GOETHE

Acceptance is the answer to *all* my problems today. If I am un-happy, it is because I am not accepting things as they are.

Discover what's doable about finding your greatness.

Embrace the "nobody" in you.

Don't forget to breathe.

Live as if you are dancing at a wedding every day.

In recovery, we learn to laugh together about things that we used to cry about while alone.

It takes more facial muscles to frown than to smile.

"Until we lose ourselves, there is no hope of finding ourselves."
—HENRY MILLER

Be an appreciator in your life. Look for what is valuable.

"Become a master at something and act like a child who knows nothing about it."
—ARTHUR MILLER

"Everybody has suffered through moments where you're thinking one thing and feeling one thing, and not showing it . . . that's acting."
—MARLON BRANDO

Always leave 'em laughing. Leave them with a joke and that's how they will remember you.

When writing comedy, throw out your best joke first.

Every "no" is one step closer to a "yes."

Surprise yourself.

"Eighty percent of success is showing up."
—WOODY ALLEN

Sandi Bachom is a producer and filmmaker living in New York City and the mother of a nineteen-year-old son. She has been in recovery for more than twenty years. After a thirty-year career in advertising and a twenty-year marriage ended, she wants you to know that it is possible to begin again at any age. She is the author of *Denial Is Not a River in Egypt* and *The Wrath of Grapes*. You can visit her Web site at www.denialqueen.com.

The headquarters of the Hazelden Foundation are in Center City, Minnesota. Additional treatment facilities are located in Chicago, Illinois; Newberg, Oregon; New York, New York; Plymouth, Minnesota; and St. Paul, Minnesota. At these sites, we provide a continuum of care for men and women of all ages. Our Plymouth facility is designed specifically for youth and families.

For more information on Hazelden, please call **1-800-257-7800.** Or you may access our World Wide Web site on the Internet at **www .hazelden.org.**

OTHER TITLES THAT MAY INTEREST YOU:

Denial Is Not a River in Egypt
Written and Edited by Sandi Bachom
Embellished with whimsical hieroglyphics, these well-chosen quotations will brighten the day of readers in any stage of recovery. Softcover, 104 pp.
Order No. 1638

The Wrath of Grapes
Written and Edited by Sandi Bachom
Filled with the timeless wit and insight of recovery slogans and quotations, *The Wrath of Grapes* reminds readers that recovering a sense of humor may be the first step toward a healthy life. Softcover, 128 pp.
Order No. 1016

Spilled Gravy
Advice on Love, Life, and Acceptance from a Man Uniquely Unqualified to Give It
Ed Driscoll
Comedian Ed Driscoll spins his everyday misadventures into amusing escapades—even finding the lighter side of alcoholism, one of the great tragedies of his life. Softcover, 208 pp.
Order No. 2610

Hazelden books are available at fine bookstores everywhere.
To order directly from Hazelden, call 1-800-328-9000 or visit www.hazelden.org/bookstore.